D0046171

Chocolate Cakes

Decadent and Delicious

Kathy Farrell-Kingsley

NEW YORK

To David—taster, critic, and best friend.
Special thanks to Nestlé Chocolate for supplying
the chocolate used to test the recipes.

A RUNNING HEADS BOOK

Copyright © 1993 by Quarto Inc.
Photographs on pages 6, 8, 14, 17, 18, 22, 24, 28, 30,
35, 38, 40, 43, 48 by Michael Harris.
Photographs on pages 5, 10, 21, 27, 33, 45 by Alan Richardson.
Photographs on pages 13, 36 courtesy of Nestlé Chocolate.

CHOCOLATE CAKES
A Running Heads book,
Quarto Inc., The Old Brewery, 6 Blundell Street, London N7 9BH

Creative Director: Linda Winters   Designer: Robbin Gourley
Senior Editor: Thomas G. Fiffer   Production Associate: Belinda Hellinger

Library of Congress Cataloging-in-Publication Data
Farrell-Kingsley, Kathy.
Chocolate cakes : decadent and delicious / Kathy Farrell-Kingsley.
—1st ed.
p.   cm.
"A Running Heads book"—T.p. verso.
ISBN 1-56282-854-1
1. Cake.   2. Cookery (Chocolate)   I. Title.
TX771.F33   1993
641.8'653—dc20   92-31065   CIP

Typeset by Trufont Typographers, Inc.
Color separations by Fine Arts Repro
Printed and bound in Hong Kong

FIRST EDITION
10   9   8   7   6   5   4   3   2   1

Contents

Wholly Chocolate

12 SERVINGS

1⅔ cups sifted cake flour

½ cup unsweetened cocoa

1 cup granulated or caster sugar

2 teaspoons baking soda

½ teaspoon salt

4 egg yolks, at room temperature

¾ cup water

¼ cup vegetable oil

1 teaspoon vanilla extract

8 egg whites, at room temperature

½ teaspoon cream of tartar

Confectioners' sugar, for dusting

1. Preheat the oven to 350° F (175° C). In a small bowl, combine the flour, cocoa, sugar, baking soda and salt.

2. In a medium-size bowl, using an electric mixer, beat the egg yolks, water, oil and vanilla on medium speed until well blended. Slowly add the flour mixture and beat for 1 minute.

3. In a large copper or stainless steel bowl, using clean beaters, beat the egg whites on high speed until foamy. Add the cream of tartar and beat on high speed until stiff peaks form. Using a rubber spatula, stir one quarter of the egg whites into the batter to lighten it. Then gently and thoroughly fold in the remaining egg whites.

4. Spoon the batter into an ungreased 10-inch (25½-cm) tube pan. Bake for 55 to 60 minutes, or until a cake tester inserted into the center comes out clean.

5. Set on a wire rack to cool for 10 minutes. Using a small metal spatula, loosen the edge of the cake from the side of the pan. Remove the cake from the pan and cool completely. Dust with confectioners' sugar before serving.

4

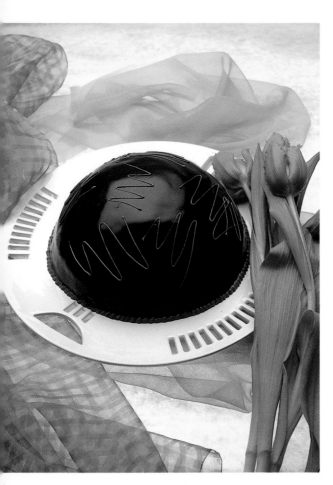

Chocolate Bombe

8 SERVINGS

½ cup cake flour

¼ cup unsweetened cocoa

4 large eggs, at room
temperature

⅔ cup granulated or caster sugar

1 tablespoon (½ ounce or 15 g)
unsalted butter, melted

3 tablespoons granulated or
caster sugar

⅓ cup water

Banana Mousse Filling (page 45)
Chocolate Ganache Glaze
(page 46)
4 ounces (115 g) semisweet
chocolate, coarsely chopped

6

1. Preheat the oven to 350° F (175° C). Grease a 1½-quart (1½-liter) stainless steel bowl. In a small bowl, sift together the flour and cocoa.

2. In a medium-size bowl, using an electric mixer, beat the eggs on medium-high speed until frothy. Slowly add the ⅔ cup of sugar and beat on high speed for 5 minutes, or until the eggs have tripled in volume and resemble soft whipped cream. Using a rubber spatula, gently and thoroughly fold in the flour mixture and the butter.

3. Pour the batter into the prepared bowl and bake for 40 to 45 minutes, or until the cake springs back when gently pressed. Set the bowl on a wire rack to cool for 5 minutes. Turn the cake out onto the rack and cool completely.

4. In a small saucepan set over moderate heat, dissolve the 3 tablespoons of sugar in the water, stirring continuously. Bring the mixture to a boil. Remove the pan from the heat.

5. Wash and dry the bowl and line with plastic wrap. Using a long, serrated knife, cut the cake horizontally into three equal pieces. Place the top piece into the prepared bowl, brush it with some of the syrup and spread with ¾ cup of the Banana Mousse Filling. Repeat with the middle piece. Brush the top side of the third piece with the remaining syrup and place it on top, then gently press the layers in place. Cover the cake with plastic wrap and chill for 2 hours.

6. Trim a cake cardboard circle to the circumference of the cake's base. Invert the cake onto the circle and place it on a wire rack set over a baking sheet. Unwrap the cake. Spread a thin layer of the Chocolate Ganache Glaze over the cake to smooth the surface, then cover it completely with the remaining glaze. Transfer to a serving platter. Chill for 10 minutes.

7. Melt the semisweet chocolate. Spoon the chocolate into a parchment cone. Cut a ¹⁄₁₆-inch (1½-mm) opening at the tip. Pipe squiggle designs on the cake and a small beaded border around the bottom edge. Chill until ready to serve.

Chocolate Sunrise

8 SERVINGS

1 ounce (30 g) semisweet chocolate, coarsely chopped

4 ounces (115 g) bittersweet chocolate, coarsely chopped

2 tablespoons (1 ounce or 30 g) unsalted butter, softened

5 large eggs, at room temperature

½ cup milk

⅓ cup granulated or caster sugar

1 teaspoon cornstarch

2 tablespoons hazelnut liqueur (optional)

1½ cups heavy or double cream

Stencil (back page)

Unsweetened cocoa, for dusting

Vanilla ice cream, for garnish

Apricot Sauce (page 46)

8

1. Line a baking sheet with parchment paper and set eight 4-inch (10-cm) round dessert rings or pastry cutters on top, spacing them 2 inches (5 cm) apart. Trace the inside of the rings onto the parchment paper, then remove the rings. Melt the semisweet chocolate and spread it in a thin layer over the traced circles. Chill the baking sheet until ready to use. Lightly grease the dessert rings or pastry cutters and set aside.

2. Melt the bittersweet chocolate and stir in the butter until melted.

3. In a double boiler set over simmering (not boiling) water, combine the eggs, milk, sugar and cornstarch. Cook, whisking continuously, for 5 to 6 minutes, or until thickened. Remove the pan from the heat. Strain the custard through a fine sieve into a medium-size bowl. Using a rubber spatula, fold the chocolate mixture into the custard. Stir in the hazelnut liqueur, if desired, and chill the mixture for 1 hour.

4. In a medium-size bowl, using an electric mixer, beat the cream on high speed until stiff peaks form, then gently and thoroughly fold it into the chilled chocolate mixture.

5. Remove the baking sheet from the refrigerator and set the prepared dessert rings over the chocolate circles. Spoon the chocolate mousse into the rings, filling them to the top edge and leveling with the straight edge of a long knife. Chill the molds for 2 hours, or until set.

6. Wrap a damp, hot cloth around the rings briefly to warm them, then remove the rings. Using a metal spatula, transfer the desserts to individual serving plates. Using a small, fine strainer, stencil the top of each dessert with cocoa. Top with ice cream and dust with cocoa.

7. Spoon the Apricot Sauce into a small parchment cone. Cut a $\frac{1}{16}$-inch ($1\frac{1}{2}$-mm) opening at the tip. Pipe six small circles of the sauce around each mousse. Using a wooden skewer, lightly draw the tip through each circle of sauce to form a heart shape. Pipe a smaller circle of the sauce between each heart shape.

Chocolate Chubbie

8 SERVINGS

1 cup all-purpose or plain flour

½ teaspoon baking powder

½ teaspoon baking soda

¼ teaspoon salt

1 stick (4 ounces or 115 g)
   unsalted butter, softened

1 cup granulated or caster sugar

2 tablespoons water

1 teaspoon vanilla extract

4 ounces (115 g) semisweet
   chocolate, coarsely chopped

4 ounces (115 g) bittersweet
   chocolate, coarsely chopped

3 large eggs

1 cup finely chopped walnuts

1 cup fresh strawberries, chopped

1½ cups heavy or double cream

1 tablespoon granulated or caster
   sugar

Whole strawberries, for garnish

Strawberry leaves, for garnish

1. Preheat the oven to 325° F (165° C). Line a 15½-by-10½-by-1-inch (39-by-26½-by-2½-cm) jelly roll pan with aluminum foil, leaving a 2-inch (5-cm) overhang on each of the ends. In a small bowl, combine the flour, baking powder, baking soda and salt.

2. In a medium-size saucepan, combine the butter, 1 cup of sugar and water. Cook, stirring frequently, over moderate heat until the sugar is dissolved and the butter is melted. Remove the pan from the heat. Stir in the vanilla and semisweet and bittersweet chocolate until melted. Transfer the chocolate mixture to a medium-size bowl and let cool.

3. Add the eggs, one at a time, stirring well after each addition. Stir in the flour mixture and the walnuts just until blended.

4. Pour the batter into the prepared pan. Bake for 15 to 18 minutes, or until a toothpick inserted into the center comes out barely clean. Set the pan on a wire rack and cool completely.

5. Purée the strawberries and strain through a fine sieve into a small bowl. In a medium-size bowl, using an electric mixer, beat the cream and 1 tablespoon of sugar on high speed until stiff peaks form. Reserve 1¼ cups of the whipped cream. Whisk the strawberry juice into the remaining whipped cream.

6. Lift the brownies out of the pan using the foil flaps for handles. Cut the brownies crosswise into eight equal strips, then cut each strip into three equal pieces. Place one brownie piece onto each of eight individual serving plates and spread each piece with some of the strawberry cream. Repeat with another layer. Top with a third brownie layer and frost the tops with the whipped cream. Garnish with fresh strawberries and strawberry leaves and serve at room temperature.

In for a Pound Chocolate

16 SERVINGS

6 ounces (170 g)
unsweetened chocolate,
coarsely chopped

2¼ cups cake flour

1 teaspoon baking soda

¾ teaspoon baking
powder

2 tablespoons instant
coffee

2 tablespoons hot water

2 sticks (8 ounces or
225 g) unsalted butter,
softened

2 cups granulated or
caster sugar

1 teaspoon vanilla extract

4 large eggs, at room
temperature

Chocolate Satin Glaze
(page 47)

Confectioners' sugar, for
dusting

1. Preheat the oven to 350° F (175° C). Grease and flour a 10-inch (25½-cm) Bundt pan or fluted tube pan.

2. Melt the chocolate. In a small bowl, combine the flour, baking soda and baking powder. In a 2-cup measure, dissolve the instant coffee in the hot water. Then, add enough cold water to measure 1½ cups.

3. In a large bowl, using an electric mixer, cream the butter with the sugar and vanilla on medium-high speed until light and fluffy. Add the eggs, one at a time, beating well after each addition. Beat in the chocolate on medium speed until well blended. Alternately beat in the coffee mixture with the flour mixture until well blended. Beat on medium-high speed for 1 minute.

4. Spoon the batter into the prepared pan. Bake for 1 hour, or until a cake tester inserted into the center comes out clean. Set the pan on a wire rack to cool for 20 minutes. Turn the cake out onto the rack and cool completely.

5. Drizzle with the Chocolate Satin Glaze and dust with the confectioners' sugar.

Nuts about Chocolate

8 SERVINGS

4 ounces (115 g) bittersweet
chocolate, coarsely chopped
2 tablespoons water
6 tablespoons cake flour
1/4 cup finely ground walnuts
4 large eggs, separated and at
room temperature
1/3 cup granulated or caster sugar
1/2 teaspoon cream of tartar

1/4 cup granulated or caster sugar
1/3 cup orange juice

Chocolate-Orange Buttercream
(page 43)
24 walnut halves, for garnish
(optional)

14

1. Preheat the oven to 350°F (175° C). Grease and flour an 8-inch (20½-cm) round cake pan. Melt the chocolate with the water. In a small bowl, combine the flour and ground walnuts.

2. In a large bowl, using an electric mixer, beat the egg yolks and the ⅓ cup of sugar on medium-high speed until thick and pale. Stir in the chocolate until well blended.

3. In a medium-size bowl, using clean beaters, beat the egg whites on high speed until foamy. Add the cream of tartar and beat on high speed until stiff peaks form. Using a rubber spatula, stir one quarter of the egg whites in the batter to lighten it. Gently and thoroughly fold in the remaining egg whites.

5. Spoon the batter into the prepared pan. Bake for 35 to 40 minutes, or until a cake tester inserted into the center comes out clean. Set the pan on a wire rack to cool for 10 minutes. Turn the cake out onto the rack and cool completely.

6. In a small saucepan, combine the ¼ cup of sugar with the orange juice. Cook, stirring occasionally, over moderate heat until the sugar is dissolved. Increase the heat to high and bring the mixture to a boil. Remove the pan from the heat.

7. Reserve 2 cups of the Chocolate-Orange Buttercream. Using a long, serrated knife, cut the cake in half horizontally. Place one half of the cake on a serving platter. Brush the surface of the cake with half of the syrup and spread with ½ cup of buttercream. Place the remaining half of the cake on top and brush with the remaining syrup. Frost the top of the cake with another ½ cup of buttercream.

8. Spoon the reserved buttercream into a pastry or piping bag fitted with a star tip. Pipe the buttercream around the side of the cake and then in a crisscross pattern over the top of the cake. Garnish the cake with the walnut halves, if desired, and serve at room temperature.

Baby Cakes

18 CUPCAKES

¾ cup unsweetened cocoa

I cup boiling water

3 large eggs, at room temperature

I teaspoon vanilla extract

2 cups all-purpose or plain flour

1½ cups granulated or caster sugar

I tablespoon baking powder

I teaspoon baking soda

½ teaspoon salt

1½ sticks (6 ounces or 170 g) unsalted butter, softened

I cup heavy or double cream

2 teaspoons granulated or caster sugar

½ teaspoon vanilla extract

Decorators' Icing (page 44)

I. Preheat the oven to 350° F (175° C). Grease eighteen standard-size muffin pan cups or line with paper liners.

2. In a medium-size bowl, combine the cocoa and water. Stir in the eggs and 1 teaspoon vanilla until well blended.

3. In a large bowl, combine the flour, 1½ cups sugar, baking powder, baking soda and salt. Using an electric mixer, beat in half of the cocoa mixture on medium speed, then the butter, then the remaining cocoa mixture. Beat on medium-high speed for 1 minute.

4. Spoon the batter into the prepared cups, filling them two thirds full. Bake for 20 to 25 minutes, or until a cake tester inserted into the center comes out clean. Set the pans on wire racks to cool for 5 minutes. Remove the cupcakes from the pans and cool completely.

5. In a medium-size bowl, using clean beaters, beat the cream, sugar and vanilla on high speed until stiff peaks form. Spoon the whipped cream into a pastry or piping bag fitted with a ⅜-inch (10-mm) plain tip. Insert the tip ¼ inch (5 mm) into the bottom of each cupcake and squeeze a little whipped cream filling into each one.

6. Spoon the Decorators' Icing into a small parchment paper cone. Cut a ¹⁄₁₆-inch (1½-mm) opening at the tip. Pipe a squiggle design on top of each cupcake.

Raspberry Dazzle

8 SERVINGS

6 ounces (170 g) semisweet
chocolate, coarsely chopped

2 sticks (8 ounces or 225 g)
unsalted butter, softened

1 cup fresh raspberries or frozen
raspberries, thawed

1½ cups granulated or caster
sugar

5 egg yolks, at room temperature

1 cup cake flour

6 egg whites, at room
temperature

2 cups raspberry liqueur

Chocolate Curls (page 47)

Confectioners' sugar, for dusting

½ recipe Crème Anglaise
(page 44)

Fresh raspberries, for garnish

1. Preheat the oven to 350° F (175° C). Lightly butter eight 6-ounce (170-g) custard cups and place them on a baking sheet. Melt the chocolate with the butter. Stir until smooth.

2. Purée the 1 cup raspberries and strain through a fine sieve into a small bowl. Stir in ¼ cup of the sugar.

3. In a large bowl, using an electric mixer, beat the egg yolks and ¾ cup of the sugar on medium-high speed until thick and pale. Stir in the chocolate mixture and the raspberry purée until well blended. Fold in the flour.

4. In a medium-size bowl, using clean beaters, beat the egg whites on high speed until foamy. Slowly add the remaining ½ cup of sugar and beat on high speed until stiff peaks form. Using a rubber spatula, stir one quarter of the egg whites into the batter to lighten it. Gently and thoroughly fold in the remaining egg whites.

5. Spoon the batter into the prepared cups, filling them half full. Bake for 20 to 25 minutes, or until a cake tester inserted into the center comes out clean. Set the custard cups on a wire rack to cool for 20 minutes. Turn the cakes out onto the rack and cool completely.

6. Pour ¼ cup of the raspberry liqueur onto each of eight individual serving plates. Place the cakes on the plates. Garnish with Chocolate Curls and dust with confectioners' sugar.

7. Spoon the Crème Anglaise into a small parchment cone. Cut a ¹⁄₁₆-inch (1½-mm) opening at the tip. Pipe the cream onto the plate as shown and garnish with the fresh raspberries.

Variation: Prepare the cake batter as directed and bake in a 9-by-13-inch (23-by-33-cm) cake pan lined with foil. Cool the cake. Lift the cake out of the pan and using a 4-inch (10-cm) round pastry cutter, cut out eight rounds of cake. Proceed as directed.

Chocolate Soufflé

6 SERVINGS

½ cup heavy or double cream

¼ cup granulated or caster sugar

5 ounces (140 g) bittersweet chocolate, coarsely chopped

5 egg yolks, at room temperature

2 tablespoons cake flour

½ teaspoon ground cinnamon

6 egg whites, at room temperature

Confectioners' sugar, for dusting

1. Preheat the oven to 425° F (220° C). Butter six 6-ounce (170-g) soufflé dishes. Place the dishes on a baking sheet.

2. In a small saucepan, bring the cream and sugar just to a boil over moderate heat and immediately remove the pan from the heat. Add the chocolate all at once and stir until the chocolate is melted and the mixture is smooth.

3. In a large bowl, using an electric mixer, beat the egg yolks and flour on medium-high speed until thick and pale. Add the chocolate mixture and cinnamon and beat on medium speed until well blended.

4. In a medium-size copper or stainless steel bowl, using clean beaters, beat the egg whites on high speed until stiff peaks form. Using a rubber spatula, stir one quarter of the egg whites into the chocolate mixture to lighten it. Then gently and thoroughly fold in the remaining egg whites.

5. Spoon the batter into the prepared dishes. Bake for 15 to 18 minutes, or until puffed.

6. Dust the soufflés with confectioners' sugar and serve immediately.

All-Frills Chocolate

16 SERVINGS

2 cups heavy or double cream

12 ounces (340 g) white
chocolate, coarsely chopped

1 ¾ cups cake flour

1 ½ teaspoons baking soda

¼ teaspoon salt

4 ounces (115 g) unsweetened
chocolate, coarsely chopped

⅔ cup (5⅓ ounces or 150 g)
unsalted butter, softened

1 ⅔ cups granulated or caster
sugar

2 teaspoons vanilla extract

3 large eggs

1 ⅓ cups milk

Dark Chocolate Glaze (page 46)

Chocolate and White Chocolate
Curls (page 47)

22

1. Preheat the oven to 350° F (175° C). Grease and flour a deep 8-inch (20½-cm) square baking pan.

2. In a medium-size saucepan, bring the cream just to a boil over moderate heat and immediately remove the pan from the heat. Add the white chocolate all at once, stirring until the chocolate is melted and the mixture is smooth. Transfer the white chocolate mixture to a medium-size bowl and chill.

3. In a small bowl, combine the flour, baking soda and salt. Melt the unsweetened chocolate.

4. In a large bowl, using an electric mixer, cream the butter with the sugar and vanilla on medium-high speed until light and fluffy. Beat in the melted chocolate on medium speed until well blended. Add the eggs, one at a time, beating well after each addition. Alternately beat in the milk and the flour mixture. Beat the batter on medium-high speed for 1 minute.

5. Pour the batter into the prepared pan. Bake for 35 to 40 minutes, or until a cake tester inserted into the center comes out clean. Set the pan on a wire rack to cool for 15 minutes. Turn the cake out onto the rack and cool completely.

6. Beat the chilled white chocolate mixture, using clean beaters, on medium-high speed just until soft peaks form. (Be careful not to overbeat or the mixture will curdle.)

7. Using a long, serrated knife, cut the cake horizontally into three equal layers. Place one layer of the cake on a serving platter and spread with half of the white chocolate filling. Repeat with the second layer and top with the remaining layer. Frost the top and side of the cake with the Dark Chocolate Glaze and decorate with the Chocolate and White Chocolate Curls.

Black Tic Chocolate

16 SERVINGS

6 ounces (170 g) semisweet
  chocolate, coarsely chopped
6 ounces (170 g) bittersweet
  chocolate, coarsely chopped
2 sticks (8 ounces or 225 g)
  unsalted butter, softened
2 cups granulated or caster sugar
6 large eggs, separated and at
  room temperature
1 cup plus 2 tablespoons cake
  flour
1 tablespoon orange liqueur
  (optional)
2 teaspoons grated orange zest
½ cup finely chopped walnuts
Dark Chocolate Glaze (page 46)
Coarsely chopped walnuts, for
  garnish
1 ounce (30 g) white chocolate,
  coarsely chopped

24

1. Preheat the oven to 350° F (175° C). Grease and flour a 9½-inch (24-cm) springform pan.

2. Melt the semisweet and bittersweet chocolate. In a large bowl, using an electric mixer, cream the butter with 1¾ cups of the sugar on medium-high speed until light and fluffy. Beat in the egg yolks until well blended. Stir in the flour, melted chocolate, orange liqueur, if desired, and orange zest.

3. In a medium-size copper or stainless steel bowl, using clean beaters, beat the egg whites on high speed until foamy. Slowly add the remaining ¼ cup sugar and beat on high speed until stiff peaks form. Using a rubber spatula, stir one quarter of the egg whites into the batter to lighten it. Then gently and thoroughly fold in the remaining egg whites. Fold in the finely chopped walnuts.

4. Pour the batter into the prepared pan. Bake for 1 hour, or until the top forms a cracked crust and the inside is moist. Set the pan on a wire rack and cool completely.

5. Remove the side of the pan from the cake. Invert the cake onto the rack and remove the pan bottom. Place a baking sheet under the rack. Pour the Dark Chocolate Glaze over the cake, covering it completely. Transfer the cake to a serving platter. Gently press the coarsely chopped walnuts into the side of the cake.

6. Melt the white chocolate and spoon it into a small parchment cone. Cut a ¹⁄₁₆-inch (1½-mm) opening at the tip. Pipe the white chocolate in a spiral design over the top of the cake. Using a wooden skewer, lightly draw alternating lines from the center of the cake to the outer edge, then from the outer edge to the center to form a spider's web pattern.

Mom's Best

12 SERVINGS

2 1/4 cups cake flour
2 teaspoons baking soda
1 3/4 cups firmly packed
  dark brown sugar
4 ounces (115 g)
  semisweet chocolate,
  coarsely chopped
1/3 cup water
2 tablespoons
  unsweetened cocoa
1 stick (4 ounces or 115 g)
  unsalted butter,
  softened
2 large eggs, at room
  temperature
2 teaspoons vanilla
  extract
1 cup buttermilk
Chocolate Buttercream
  (page 42)

1. Preheat the oven to 350° F (175° C). Grease and flour two deep 8-inch (20½-cm) round cake pans. In a small bowl, combine the flour and baking soda.

2. In a medium-size saucepan, combine the sugar, chocolate and water. Bring the mixture to a boil over moderate heat, stirring frequently. Remove the pan from the heat. Stir in the cocoa and butter until the butter is melted and the mixture is smooth. Transfer the mixture to a large bowl and cool to room temperature.

3. Using an electric mixer, beat the eggs and vanilla into the chocolate mixture on medium speed until well blended. Alternately beat in the flour mixture and buttermilk. Beat on medium-high speed for 1 minute.

4. Pour the batter into the prepared pans. Bake for 25 to 30 minutes, or until a cake tester inserted into the center comes out clean. Set the pans on wire racks to cool for 15 minutes. Turn the cakes out onto the racks and cool completely.

5. Place one cake layer on a serving platter and spread with one-third of the Chocolate Buttercream. Top with the second cake layer and frost the top and side with the remaining buttercream.

26

Luscious Layers

16 SERVINGS

2 sticks (8 ounces or 225 g) unsalted butter, softened

¾ cup granulated or caster sugar

8 large eggs, separated and at room temperature

3 tablespoons water

2 tablespoons unsweetened cocoa

4 cups chocolate cake crumbs (see note opposite) *

¼ teaspoon salt

1 teaspoon baking soda

¾ cup heavy or double cream

6 ounces (170 g) bittersweet chocolate, coarsely chopped

Chocolate Curls (page 47)

28

1. Preheat the oven to 350° F (175° C). Line a 15½-by-10½-by-1-inch (39-by-26½-by-2½-cm) jelly roll pan with parchment paper.

2. In a large bowl, using an electric mixer, cream the butter with ½ cup of the sugar on medium-high speed until light and fluffy. Beat in the egg yolks, water and cocoa until well blended.

3. In a medium-size copper or stainless steel bowl, using clean beaters, beat the egg whites on high speed until foamy. Slowly add the remaining ¼ cup of sugar and beat on high speed until stiff peaks form. Using a rubber spatula, alternately fold the cake crumbs and egg whites into the chocolate mixture until well blended. Stir in the salt and baking soda.

4. Spread the batter evenly into the prepared pan. Bake for 20 to 25 minutes, or until the cake springs back when gently pressed. Set the pan on a wire rack to cool for 5 minutes. Turn the cake out onto a baking sheet, remove the parchment paper and cool completely.

5. In a small saucepan, bring the cream just to a boil over moderate heat and immediately remove the pan from the heat. Add the chocolate all at once and stir until the chocolate is melted and the mixture is smooth. Transfer the mixture to a small bowl and chill for 45 minutes. Using clean beaters, beat the chilled chocolate mixture on high speed until stiff peaks form. Reserve ⅓ cup of the chocolate filling.

6. Cut the cake crosswise into three equal sections. Place the first layer on a serving platter. Spread with half of the chocolate filling. Repeat with the second layer, place the remaining cake layer on top and spread with the reserved filling. Using a long, sharp knife, neatly trim all four sides of the assembled cake. Garnish with Chocolate Curls.

Note: Place the equivalent of two store-bought 8-inch (20½-cm) round chocolate cakes into a food processor fitted with the metal blade and process to fine crumbs.

Truffle Tart

12 SERVINGS

1½ cups graham cracker crumbs

2 teaspoons ground cinnamon

¼ cup (2 ounces or 55 g) unsalted butter, melted

8 ounces (225 g) white chocolate, coarsely chopped

1 8-ounce (225-g) package cream cheese, softened

2 tablespoons honey

2 large eggs, at room temperature

1 cup heavy or double cream

3 ounces (85 g) semisweet chocolate, coarsely chopped

1. Preheat the oven to 325° F (165° C).

2. In a small bowl, combine the graham cracker crumbs, cinnamon and melted butter until well blended. Firmly press the mixture into the side and bottom of a 9-inch (23-cm) pie pan. Chill the pie crust until ready to use.

3. Melt the white chocolate. In a medium-size bowl, using an electric mixer, beat the cream cheese and honey on medium-high speed until light and fluffy. Beat in the white chocolate on medium speed. Using a rubber spatula, occasionally scrape down the side of the bowl. Add the eggs, one at a time, beating well after each addition. Beat in the cream. Beat the mixture on medium-high speed until smooth.

4. Pour the batter into the prepared crust. Bake for 25 to 30 minutes, or until the center is just set. Transfer the pan to a wire rack and cool completely. Chill the pie for 2 to 3 hours.

5. Melt the semisweet chocolate and spoon it into a small parchment cone. Cut a ¹⁄₁₆-inch (1½-mm) opening at the tip. Pipe ten parallel lines across the surface of the pie, spacing them about ½ inch (1½ cm) apart. Using the tip of a wooden skewer, lightly draw perpendicular lines through the piping at ½-inch (1½-cm) intervals to create a marbled pattern.

Festooned with Fruit

12 SERVINGS

2 cups cake flour

2 cups granulated or
caster sugar

½ cup unsweetened cocoa

1 teaspoon baking soda

1 teaspoon ground allspice

½ teaspoon ground ginger

½ teaspoon ground nutmeg

¼ teaspoon ground cloves

½ teaspoon salt

¾ cup vegetable oil

¾ cup buttermilk

2 large eggs, at room
temperature

¾ cup boiling water

1½ cups heavy or double
cream

1 tablespoon
confectioners' sugar

1 teaspoon vanilla extract

1 pint fresh raspberries

Mint leaves, for garnish

Unsweetened cocoa, for
dusting

1. Preheat the oven to 350° F (175° C). Grease and flour two 8-inch (20½-cm) round cake pans.

2. In a large bowl, combine the flour, granulated sugar, cocoa, baking soda, spices and salt. Using an electric mixer, beat in the oil, buttermilk and eggs on medium speed until well blended. Slowly add the water and beat on medium speed for 1 minute.

3. Pour the batter into the prepared pans. Bake for 30 to 35 minutes, or until a cake tester inserted into the center comes out clean. Set the pans on wire racks to cool for 15 minutes. Turn the cakes out onto the racks and cool completely.

4. In a medium-size bowl, using clean beaters, beat the cream, confectioners' sugar and vanilla on high speed until stiff peaks form.

5. Place one cake layer on a serving platter and spread with half of the whipped cream and one third of the raspberries. Place the second cake layer on top and press gently. Top with the remaining whipped cream. Garnish with another one third of the raspberries and mint leaves. Dust the surface with cocoa and serve with the remaining raspberries.

32

Solid Chocolate

16 SERVINGS

9 ounces (225 g)
  semisweet chocolate,
  coarsely chopped
3 ounces (85 g)
  unsweetened chocolate,
  coarsely chopped
2½ sticks (10 ounces or
  285 g) unsalted butter,
  softened
9 large eggs, separated
  and at room
  temperature
1¼ cups granulated or
  caster sugar
1 cup cake flour
1 teaspoon cream of
  tartar
Chocolate Satin Glaze
  (page 47)
Chocolate Curls (page 47)
Chocolate Circles
  (page 48)
Confectioners' sugar,
  for dusting

1. Preheat the oven to 350° F (175° C). Grease and flour a 9½-inch (24-cm) springform pan. Melt the semisweet and unsweetened chocolate with the butter. Transfer to a large bowl.

2. In a medium-size bowl, using an electric mixer, beat the egg yolks on medium-high speed with the granulated sugar. Stir the egg yolk mixture into the chocolate. Add the flour and stir until well blended.

3. In a medium-size copper or stainless steel bowl, using clean beaters, beat the egg whites on high speed until foamy. Add the cream of tartar and beat on high speed until stiff peaks form. Using a rubber spatula, stir one quarter of the egg whites into the batter to lighten it. Gently and thoroughly fold in the remaining egg whites.

4. Pour the batter into the prepared pan. Bake for 45 to 55 minutes, or until the top feels barely firm to the touch. Set the pan on a rack and cool completely.

5. Remove the side of the pan from the cake. Invert the cake onto a serving platter and remove the pan bottom. Frost the top and side of the cake with the Chocolate Satin Glaze. Decorate with the Chocolate Curls and Chocolate Circles. Dust the top with confectioners' sugar.

Midnight Torte

12 SERVINGS

6 ounces (170 g)
  semisweet chocolate
  chips
1¼ cups water
2¼ cups all-purpose or
  plain flour
1 teaspoon baking soda
½ teaspoon salt
1½ sticks (6 ounces or
  170 g) unsalted butter,
  softened
1½ cups granulated or
  caster sugar
1 teaspoon vanilla extract
3 large eggs, at room
  temperature
2 cups heavy or double
  cream
¼ cup unsweetened cocoa,
  sifted
¼ cup confectioners'
  sugar, sifted
Dark Chocolate Glaze
  (page 46)

1. Preheat the oven to 375° F (190° C). Grease and flour two 9-inch (23-cm) round cake pans.

2. Melt the chocolate chips with ¼ cup of the water. In a small bowl, combine the flour, baking soda and salt.

3. In a large bowl, using an electric mixer, cream the butter with the granulated sugar and vanilla on medium-high speed until light and fluffy. Add the eggs, one at a time, beating well after each addition. Beat in the chocolate. Alternately beat in the flour mixture and the remaining 1 cup of water on medium speed until well blended.

4. Pour the batter into the prepared pans. Bake for 30 to 35 minutes, or until a cake tester inserted into the center comes out clean. Set the pans on wire racks to cool for 10 minutes. Turn the cakes out onto the racks and cool completely.

5. In a small bowl, using clean beaters, beat the cream, cocoa and confectioners' sugar on high speed until stiff peaks form.

6. Using a long, serrated knife, split each cake layer in half horizontally. Place one split cake layer on a serving platter and spread with ⅓ cup of the whipped cream filling. Repeat with remaining layers and filling. Frost the top and side with the Dark Chocolate Glaze.

Oodles of Chocolate

12 SERVINGS

1 ounce (30 g) semisweet
   chocolate, coarsely chopped
6 ounces (170 g) milk chocolate,
   coarsely chopped
3¾ cups heavy or double cream
12 ounces (340 g) white
   chocolate, coarsely chopped
⅓ cup canned chestnut purée
   (optional)
Chocolate Clay (page 48)
8 shelled whole chestnuts, for
   garnish (optional)

38

1. Trace the bottom of an 8½-inch (21½-cm) springform pan onto parchment paper. Cut out the circle and tape the edges to a baking sheet to prevent it from curling.

2. Melt the semisweet chocolate and spread it in a thin layer over the parchment circle. Chill until the chocolate is firm. Peel off the parchment paper and set the chocolate circle on the bottom of the springform pan.

3. Melt the milk chocolate and transfer it to a medium-size bowl. In another medium-size bowl, using an electric mixer, beat 1¼ cups of the cream on high speed until stiff peaks form. Using a rubber spatula, stir one quarter of the whipped cream into the milk chocolate to lighten it. Gently and thoroughly fold in the remaining whipped cream. Spoon the milk chocolate mixture into the prepared pan and level with a metal spatula. Wipe the inside of the pan clean above the milk chocolate mixture.

4. Melt the white chocolate and transfer it to a large bowl. Stir in the chestnut purée, if desired. In a medium-size bowl, using clean beaters, beat the remaining 2½ cups of cream on high speed until stiff peaks form. Stir one quarter of the whipped cream into the white chocolate to lighten it. Gently and thoroughly fold in the remaining whipped cream. Spoon the white chocolate mixture over the milk chocolate mixture and level with a metal spatula. Chill for 4 to 6 hours, or until set.

5. Wrap a damp, hot cloth briefly around the side of the pan to warm it, then release the side of the pan. Transfer the dessert to a serving platter. Garnish with strands of the Chocolate Clay and whole chestnuts, if desired, and serve chilled.

Almond Delight

12 SERVINGS

10 ounces (285 g) semisweet chocolate, coarsely chopped

2 sticks (8 ounces or 225 g) unsalted butter, softened

1 cup granulated or caster sugar

6 large eggs, separated and at room temperature

2 tablespoons apricot preserves

2 tablespoons orange liqueur

1 cup finely ground almonds

1 cup cake flour

1 cup fresh or frozen raspberries, thawed

¼ cup confectioners' sugar, sifted

Crème Anglaise (page 44)

Confectioners' sugar, for dusting

Sliced unblanched almonds, for garnish

Apricot Sauce (page 46)

1. Preheat the oven to 350° F (175° C). Line a 15½-by-10½-by-1-inch (39-by-26½-by-2½-cm) jelly roll pan with parchment paper. Lightly grease the parchment paper. Melt the chocolate.

2. In a large bowl, using an electric mixer, cream the butter with ¾ cup of the granulated sugar on medium-high speed until light and fluffy. Beat in the egg yolks, apricot preserves, orange liqueur and melted chocolate on medium speed until well blended.

3. In a small bowl, combine the ground almonds and flour.

4. In a medium-size bowl, using clean beaters, beat the egg whites on high speed until foamy. Slowly add the remaining ¼ cup of granulated sugar and beat on high speed until stiff peaks form. Using a rubber spatula, stir one quarter of the egg whites into the batter to lighten it. Alternately fold in the remaining egg whites and the flour mixture.

5. Spoon the batter into the prepared pan. Bake for 18 to 20 minutes, or until the cake springs back when gently pressed. Set the pan on a wire rack to cool for 15 minutes. Turn the cake out onto a baking sheet, remove the parchment paper and cool completely.

6. Purée the raspberries and strain through a fine sieve into a small bowl. Stir in the ¼ cup of confectioners' sugar.

7. Using a 3-inch (7½-cm) round biscuit cutter, cut out twelve rounds of cake. Spoon equal amounts of the Crème Anglaise onto twelve individual serving plates. Place the cake rounds on top of the sauce. Dust the rounds with confectioners' sugar and arrange three sliced almonds on top.

8. Spoon the raspberry purée and Apricot Sauce into two separate small parchment cones. Cut a ¹⁄₁₆-inch (1½-mm) opening at each tip. Alternately pipe small circles of the apricot sauce and the raspberry purée onto the Crème Anglaise around each cake. Using a wooden skewer, lightly draw the tip through each circle of sauce to form a heart shape.

All the Extras

Chocolate Melting Directions

Semisweet and Bittersweet Chocolate: Place the coarsely chopped chocolate in the top of a double boiler set over simmering (not boiling) water and stir until the chocolate is melted and smooth.

Microwave Directions: Place the coarsely chopped chocolate in a dry, microwave-safe bowl. Microwave on High (100 percent power) for 1 minute. Stir and microwave on Medium (50 percent power) for 30 seconds. Stir and microwave on Medium for 30 seconds more, or until melted and smooth.

White and Milk Chocolate: Place the coarsely chopped chocolate in a bowl set in hot tap water. Let stand, stirring occasionally, until melted and smooth.

Microwave Directions: Place the coarsely chopped chocolate in a dry microwave-safe bowl. Microwave on Low (20 percent power) for 2 minutes. Stir and microwave on Low for 2 minutes. Stir and microwave on Low for 1 minute more, or until melted and smooth.

Chocolate Buttercream

3 1⁄2 CUPS

2 ounces (55 g) unsweetened chocolate, coarsely chopped
2 ounces (55 g) semisweet chocolate, coarsely chopped
1 1⁄2 sticks (6 ounces or 170 g) unsalted butter, softened
2 teaspoons vanilla extract
6 cups confectioners' sugar, sifted
1⁄2 cup buttermilk or milk

1. Melt the unsweetened and semisweet chocolate and cool to room temperature.

2. In a medium-size bowl, using an elec-

42

tric mixer, beat the butter on medium-high speed until light and fluffy. Reduce speed to medium and beat in the chocolate and vanilla. Alternately beat in the confectioners' sugar and buttermilk or milk until the icing reaches a spreading consistency. Beat on medium-high speed until smooth.

Coffee Buttercream: Omit the unsweetened and semisweet chocolate and the buttermilk. Dissolve 1 tablespoon instant espresso in $\frac{1}{2}$ cup of hot water and let cool to room temperature. Proceed as directed.

Chocolate-Orange Buttercream

3 CUPS
6 egg yolks
¾ cup granulated or caster sugar
4 ounces (115 g) semisweet
   chocolate, coarsely chopped
½ cup orange juice
3 sticks (12 ounces or 340 g)
   unsalted butter, softened and
   cut in small pieces

1. In a double boiler set over simmering (not boiling) water, combine the egg yolks, sugar, chocolate and orange juice. Cook, stirring frequently, until the chocolate is melted and the sugar is dissolved. Transfer the mixture to a large bowl and let cool.

2. Using an electric mixer, beat the cooled chocolate mixture on medium-high speed for 1 minute. Slowly beat in the butter until light and fluffy.

43

Decorators' Icing

½ CUP

I tablespoon egg white, at room
  temperature
¾ cup confectioners' sugar, sifted

In a medium-size bowl, using an electric
mixer, beat the egg white and confectioners' sugar on medium-low speed until
the sugar is moistened. Increase speed to
high and beat until the icing is glossy and
stiff peaks form.

Crème Anglaise

2 ½ CUPS

6 egg yolks
½ cup granulated or caster sugar
2 cups milk
I teaspoon vanilla extract

I. In a medium-size bowl, using an electric mixer, beat the egg yolks and sugar on
medium-high speed until thick and pale.

2. In a medium-size saucepan, bring the
milk just to a boil and immediately remove
the pan from the heat. Slowly whisk the
milk into the egg yolk mixture and then
return to the saucepan. Cook, whisking
continuously, over medium-low heat, for
10 to 12 minutes, or until the custard has
thickened slightly and lightly coats the
back of a spoon. Remove the pan from the
heat. Stir in the vanilla. Strain the custard
through a fine sieve into a small bowl.
Cool to room temperature. Cover the surface of the sauce with plastic wrap and
chill for 1 hour.

44

Banana Mousse Filling

2 1/4 CUPS

3 egg yolks
1/3 cup granulated or caster sugar
1/2 cup milk
2 teaspoons unflavored gelatin
2 tablespoons water
I ripe banana, mashed (1/2 cup)
1/2 teaspoon vanilla extract
3/4 cup heavy or double cream

I. In a small bowl, using an electric mixer, beat the egg yolks and sugar on medium-high speed until thick and pale. In a small saucepan, bring the milk to a boil and immediately remove the pan from the heat. Slowly whisk the milk into the egg yolk mixture and then return to the saucepan. Cook, whisking continuously, over medium-low heat until the custard has thickened slightly and lightly coats the back of a spoon. Transfer the mixture to a medium-size bowl.

2. In a small bowl, sprinkle the gelatin over the water and let stand for 1 minute to soften. Stir the gelatin, banana and vanilla into the custard until well blended. Cool to room temperature.

3. In a medium-size bowl, using clean beaters, beat the cream on high speed until stiff peaks form. Using a rubber spatula, gently and thoroughly fold the whipped cream into the banana mixture. Chill until ready to use.

Chocolate Ganache Glaze

2 1/4 CUPS

8 ounces (225 g) bittersweet or
  semisweet chocolate, coarsely
  chopped
1 cup heavy or double cream
3 tablespoons light corn syrup
1 teaspoon vanilla extract

Place the chocolate in a small bowl. In a small saucepan, bring the cream and corn syrup just to a boil over moderate heat and immediately remove the pan from the heat. Pour the hot cream mixture over the chocolate and let stand for 1 minute. Stir until the chocolate is melted and the mixture is smooth. Stir in the vanilla. Let the glaze cool slightly.

Apricot Sauce

1 CUP

1 1/4 cups water
1/2 cup apricot brandy
2 tablespoons lemon juice
1/4 cup granulated or caster sugar
1/3 cup dried apricots, chopped

In a medium-size saucepan, combine the water, brandy, lemon juice and sugar. Cook, stirring frequently, over moderate heat until the sugar is dissolved. Increase the heat to medium-high and bring the mixture to a boil. Add the apricots, reduce the heat to medium-low, and cook, stirring occasionally, for 30 minutes. Transfer the mixture to a blender or a food processor fitted with the metal blade and purée. Strain the sauce through a fine sieve into a small bowl and cool.

Dark Chocolate Glaze

1 2/3 CUPS

1/2 stick (2 ounces or 55 g)
  unsalted butter, softened
3 tablespoons light corn syrup
2 tablespoons water
8 ounces (225 g) bittersweet
  chocolate, coarsely chopped

In a small saucepan, combine the butter, corn syrup and water. Bring the mixture just to a boil, stirring frequently, over moderate heat. Remove the pan from the heat. Add the chocolate all at once, stirring until the chocolate is melted and the mixture is smooth. Transfer the glaze to a small bowl and cool slightly.

Chocolate Satin Glaze

1 1/2 CUPS

6 ounces (170 g) semisweet
  chocolate, coarsely chopped
1/2 cup heavy or double cream
2 tablespoons confectioners'
  sugar
1 teaspoon vanilla extract
2 teaspoons dark rum (optional)

In a medium-size saucepan, combine the chocolate, cream, confectioners' sugar and vanilla. Cook, stirring frequently, over medium-low heat, until the chocolate is melted and the mixture is smooth. Remove the pan from the heat. Stir in the

rum, if desired. Transfer the glaze to a small bowl and cool slightly.

Chocolate Curls

6 ounces (170 g) dark, white or
  milk chocolate, melted

1. Using a metal spatula, spread the melted chocolate evenly, about $\frac{1}{16}$ inch (1½ mm) thick, over the back of a 12-by-18-inch (30½-by-46-cm) baking pan or baking sheet. Chill for at least 20 minutes, or until the chocolate is firm. Remove the pan from the refrigerator and warm to room temperature, or until the chocolate is soft enough to scrape.

2. Hold a metal spatula at a 45-degree angle with the pan and scrape the chocolate from the surface to form curls. (If the chocolate cracks or splinters as you scrape, it is still too cold. If the chocolate melts against the spatula, it is too warm and should be chilled again briefly.) Chill the curls until ready to use.

47

Chocolate Circles: Line a baking sheet with waxed or greaseproof paper. Melt the chocolate and spread it evenly, $\frac{1}{16}$ inch ($1\frac{1}{2}$ mm) thick, over the waxed paper. Chill until softly set but not hard. Using a 2-inch (5-cm) round pastry or cookie cutter, cut circles out of the chocolate. Return the baking sheet to the refrigerator and chill until firm. Gently remove the circles from the wax paper.

Note: Chocolate curls and circles can be made up to two weeks ahead. Refrigerate between sheets of waxed or greaseproof paper in an airtight container.

Chocolate Clay

14 ounces (400 g) milk chocolate
⅓ cup light corn syrup

1. Line a baking sheet with waxed or greaseproof paper. Melt the chocolate. In a medium-size bowl, mix the melted chocolate and corn syrup just until blended. (Do not overmix or the chocolate will separate.) Pour the mixture onto the prepared baking sheet and, using a metal spatula, spread the mixture into a 6-inch (15-cm) square. Let the mixture stand at room temperature for several hours, or until the dough is the consistency of modeling clay. Knead the dough until it becomes smooth and pliable (it may seem hard and crumbly at first).

2. Divide the dough into ten equal pieces and flatten each piece into a disk. Run each disk through a pasta machine a few times to flatten further. Run the flattened pieces of dough through the spaghetti cutter to form chocolate strands.

Stencil for Chocolate Sunrise

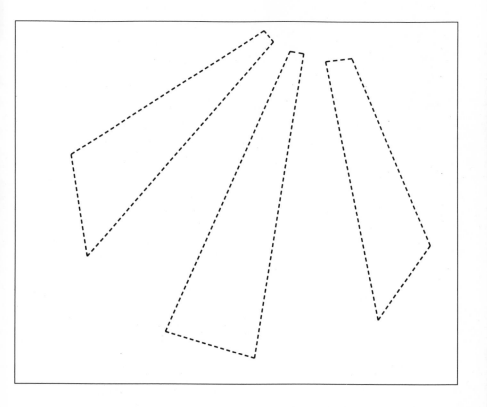